A Day in the Life: Rainforest Animals

Tarantula

Anita Ganeri

www.raintreepublishers.co.uk
Visit our website to find out
more information about
Raintree books.

To order:
☎ Phone 0845 6044371
🖷 Fax +44 (0) 1865 312263
🖳 Email myorders@raintreepublishers.co.uk

Customers from outside the UK please telephone +44 1865 312262

Raintree is an imprint of Capstone Global Library Limited,
a company incorporated in England and Wales having its
registered office at 7 Pilgrim Street, London, EC4V 6LB –
Registered company number: 6695582

Text © Capstone Global Library Limited 2011
First published in hardback in 2011
The moral rights of the proprietor have been asserted.

Edited by Nancy Dickmann, Rebecca Rissman,
   and Catherine Veitch
Designed by Steve Mead
Picture research by Mica Brancic
Originated by Capstone Global Library
Printed and bound in China by South China Printing
   Company Ltd

ISBN 978 1 4062 1788 9 (hardback)
14 13 12 11 10
10 9 8 7 6 5 4 3 2 1

British Library Cataloguing in Publication Data
Ganeri, Anita
Tarantula. -- (A day in the life. Rainforest animals)
595.4'4-dc22
A full catalogue record for this book is available from the
British Library.

Acknowledgements
We would like to thank the following for permission to
reproduce photographs: Ardea **pp. 6**, **23 fang** (Andy Teare);
Corbis **pp. 7** (© David A. Northcott), **14**, **23 silk** (© Michael
& Patricia Fogden), **20** (© Radius Images); FLPA **pp. 9**, **17**, **23
exoskeleton** (Minden Pictures/Mark Moffett), **11** (Minden
Pictures/James Christensen); Photolibrary **pp. 4** (age fotostock/
John Cancalosi), **5** (Oxford Scientific (OSF)/John Mitchell), **12**,
15, **23 prey**, **23 spiderling** (Oxford Scientific (OSF)/Emanuele
Biggi), **13**, **16** (Oxford Scientific (OSF)/Nick Gordon), **22**
(Oxford Scientific (OSF)/Robert Oelman); Photoshot **pp. 10**,
23 burrow (NHPA), **18** (NHPA/Jany Sauvanet), **19** (NHPA/
Daniel Heuclin), **21** (© NHPA/George Bernard); Shutterstock
p. 23 rainforest (© Szefei).

Cover photograph of a South American zebra
tarantula reproduced with permission of Shutterstock
(worldswildlifewonders).

Back cover photographs of (left) a tarantula's burrow
reproduced with permission of FLPA (Minden Pictures/
Mark Moffett); and (right) a tarantula spiderling reproduced
with permission of Photolibrary (Oxford Scientific (OSF)/
Emanuele Biggi).

We would like to thank Michael Bright for his invaluable help
in the preparation of this book.

Every effort has been made to contact copyright holders
of material reproduced in this book. Any omissions will
be rectified in subsequent printings if notice is given to
the publisher.

Contents

Some words are in bold, **like this**. You can find them in the glossary on page 23.

What is a tarantula?

Tarantulas are very big spiders.

All spiders have eight legs and their bodies are divided into two parts.

Goliath bird-eater

There are many different types of tarantula.

The largest type of tarantula is called the Goliath bird-eater.

What do tarantulas look like?

fang

Tarantulas have large, round bodies.

They have strong jaws with poisonous **fangs**.

eyes

A tarantula has a group of tiny eyes on the top of its head.

Its body and legs are covered in tiny hairs.

Where do tarantulas live?

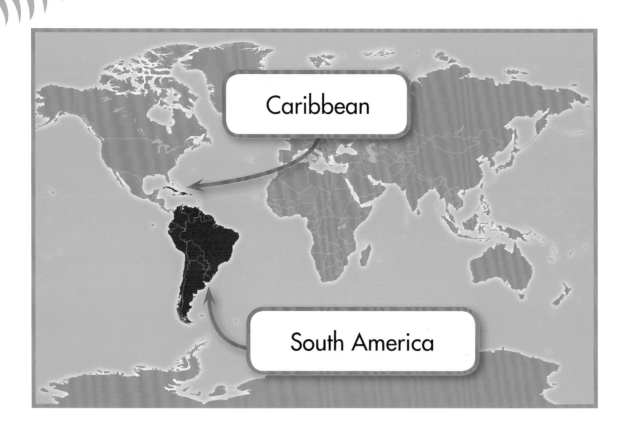

Caribbean

South America

Many tarantulas live in the **rainforests** of South America and the Caribbean.

It is warm and wet in the rainforests.

burrow

Some tarantulas live on the forest floor, under rocks or logs.

Others dig **burrows** in the ground.

What do tarantulas do at night?

At night, a tarantula leaves its **burrow** to look for food.

It crawls slowly across the forest floor but it does not travel very far.

Then the tarantula waits for its **prey** to come near.

It grabs its prey and kills it with a bite from its poisonous **fangs**.

What do tarantulas eat?

frog

Tarantulas mainly eat **rainforest** insects and other spiders.

They can also catch frogs, snakes, small lizards, and small birds.

After a good meal, a tarantula does not need to eat again for a whole month.

It sits in its **burrow** until it needs to go hunting again.

Where are baby tarantulas born?

eggs inside a silk bag

Baby tarantulas are born in a **burrow** at night.

The female lays hundreds of eggs and wraps them in a **silk** bag.

spiderling

The female guards the eggs until the **spiderlings** hatch.

The spiderlings leave the burrow when they are about two weeks old.

How do tarantulas grow?

exoskeleton

A tarantula has a hard skin around its body called an **exoskeleton**.

As the tarantula grows bigger, its skin becomes too tight.

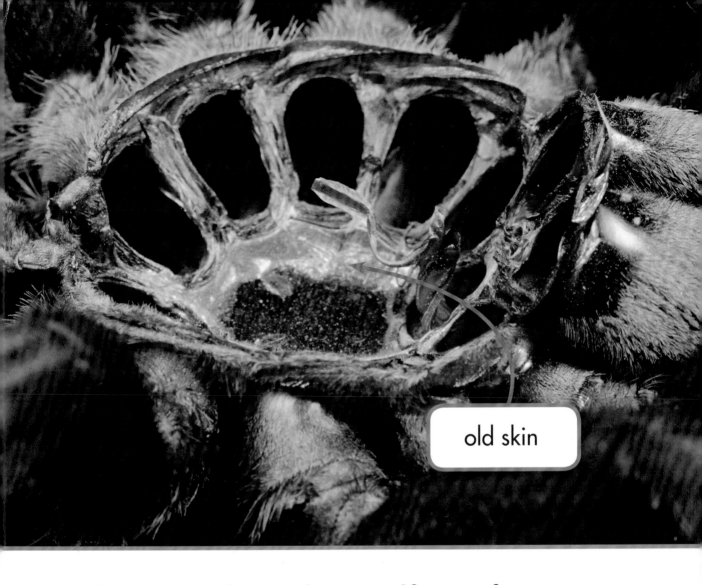

old skin

The tarantula pushes itself out of its old skin.

It has a new, bigger skin underneath.

What do tarantulas do in the day?

burrow

In the day, a tarantula rests in its **burrow**.

It does not sleep in the same way as you do.

hairs

If the tarantula is disturbed, it gives a loud hiss.

Then it flicks hairs from its body into its attacker's face.

What hunts tarantulas?

grilled tarantulas

Rainforest animals, such as lizards, snakes, and birds, hunt tarantulas to eat.

People also eat tarantulas.

hawk wasp

Hawk wasps hunt tarantulas as they rest during the day.

A wasp stings a spider to stop it moving. It uses the spider as food for its young.

Tarantula body map

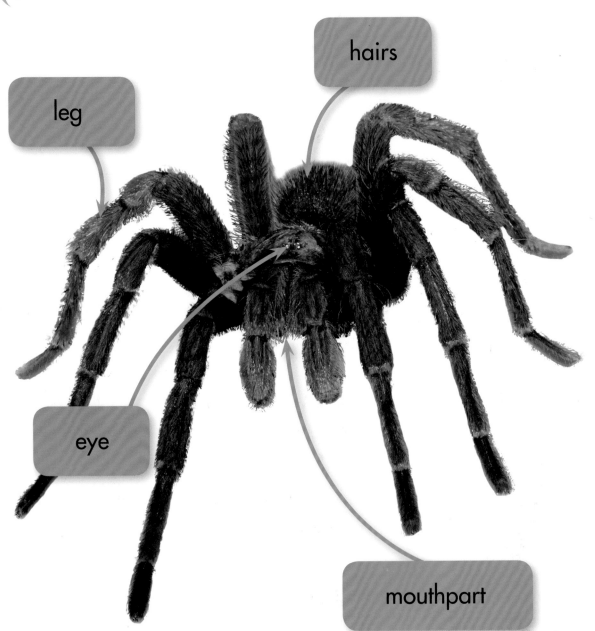

hairs

leg

eye

mouthpart

Glossary

 **burrow** hole in the ground that animals live in

 **exoskeleton** hard skin around a spider's body

 **fang** sharp body part like a tooth. It squeezes out poison.

 **prey** animal that is hunted by other animals for food

 **rainforest** thick forest with very tall trees and a lot of rain

 **silk** soft, strong material made by spiders and other minibeasts

 **spiderling** baby spider

Find out more

Books

Do Tarantulas Have Teeth? Questions and Answers about Poisonous Creatures, Melvin Berger (Scholastic, 2007)

Usborne Beginners: Rainforest, Lucy Beckett-Bowman (Usborne, 2008)

Websites

http://animals.nationalgeographic.com/animals/bugs/tarantula.html

www.arkive.org [search tarantula]

http://a-z-animals.com/animals/red-knee-tarantula/

Index